Gwathmey Siegel

Gwathmey
Siegel

Buildings and Projects
1965–2000

Introduction by Charles Gwathmey
Edited by Brad Collins

Universe editor: Richard Olsen
Copy editor: Iris Becker

First published in the United States of America in 2000
by UNIVERSE PUBLISHING
A Division of Rizzoli International
300 Park Avenue South, New York, New York 10010

00 01 02 03 / 10 9 8 7 6 5 4 3 2 1

Library of Congress Cataloging-in-Publication Data
Gwathmey Siegel: buildings and projects 1965–2000/edited by Brad Collins;
introduction by Charles Gwathmey.
p.cm.
ISBN 0-7893-0401-5 (pbk).
1. Gwathmey Siegel & Associates Architects. 2. Architecture, Modern–20th
century–United States. 3. Architecture, Postmodern–United States. I. Collins, Brad.

NA737.G95 G84 2000
720'.92'2–dc21

00-020544

front cover: IBM Corporate Office and Distribution Building (lower left), photo by Richard Bryant/Arcaid;
Levitt Center for University Advancement, University of Iowa, photo byAssassi Productions.
Stadtportalhäuser, plan
back cover: San Onofre Residence (upper left), photo by Assassi Productions;
Solomon R. Guggenheim Renovation and Addition, photo by Jeff Goldberg/Esto.

Design and type composition by Group C Inc NEW HAVEN | BOSTON (BC, MM, EZ)

Printed in Italy

Contents

Introduction

CHARLES GWATHMEY

Design is a discovery process. It is a formal investigation of ideas and strategies that results in a work that transcends accommodation. As a process, it is essentially reductive and interrogative. If resolved holistically, the aesthetic is inherent and unreplicative.

The work presented in this volume documents this process as a sequence of investigations that informs all of our work. It is a process of growing, refining, and changing. We start with the residences because they are, at a certain level, formal and prototypical studies representing an ideal. They are ideograms and microcosms of an interpretation of architecture. They are laboratories for developing strategies that are universal rather than idiosyncratic. Ideally, they are paradigms.

Given the condensed and composite nature of this monograph, one can trace the development of certain ideas and strategies within one building type, and then decipher the influence of one building type on another as a continuous investigation of our process.

In the Gwathmey Residence and Studio, designed for my parents in 1965, I had the opportunity, at the very beginning of my career, to articulate ideas relating to volume, form, intersection, and light. Beginning, conceptually, with a solid, then carving, eroding, and reducing the building to an essence of solid and void, resulting in a site-defining sculptural object. The siting of the house and studio established a dialogue of rotation—facade to corner—that altered the singular site–object relationship and created an enriched sense of place.

In the Cogan Residence, designed in 1970, we were given a site and program that were of a different scale and size than any of our previous projects. There was not just the opportunity, but the obligation to reevaluate our formal intentions. Up until that point, the object, per se—a carved, eroded, geometric form—was primary and singular. Simply expanding the vocabulary and partis of the first series of houses was problematic. Extending the strategy would lose the essence, compositeness, and clarity of the object.

In Cogan, for the first time the "object building," with its sculptural representation, was combined with a more universal referential pavilion. The object building was locked into a rectilinear frame structure and extended horizontally and vertically through it. We had discovered a new formal and organizational strategy for manipulating scale and articulating separate elements that were intended to be read as engaged yet contrapuntal, rather than as singular or consolidated. Hierarchically and formally, the two elements not only coexist but also enrich and inform one another spatially, volumetrically, and formally.

While we were realizing the Cogan Residence, we were simultaneously designing Whig Hall at Princeton University, a neoclassical replication that had been gutted by fire, leaving only the marble exterior walls. Our solution was to create a modern intervention—a new object—that was structurally and aesthetically independent. By removing the existing east wall, we revealed the archetypal single space defined by the original frame and animated it by inserting the "new object," in obvious historical and compositional counterpoint to the classical form and language of the original structure. With Cogan we created the frame; with Whig we "found" the frame.

The de Menil Residence, designed in 1979, can be read as a layering of frames that articulate a sequence of spatial zones. These zones, defined by their internal facades and their sectional manipulation, establish a dense horizontal and vertical spatial interlocking that is enriched by transparency. This strategy established the idea of a volume, rather than a plane, as wall.

The brise-soleil articulates the south facade layer that faces the dune and the ocean, and is incorporated into the layering. As a frame, it accommodates a series of spatial articulations: screened porch, breakfast room, master bathroom, as well as terraces and decks.

The entry zone, or north facade layer, faces back to the land and is animated by the volume and presence of the three-and-a-half-story greenhouse, which is read as the primary vertical space from both the exterior and interior. The greenhouse is designed as an object, extending beyond the frame of the roof, and as a spatial frame modulated by the intervention of the study balcony. The strategy of multiple frames and volumes acting simultaneously as spatial layers and objects is a significant extension and elaboration of the object/frame strategy first discovered in Cogan.

In the addition to the Guggenheim Museum, designed in 1982, the condition was the opposite of Whig Hall, where the frame had been a given. With the Guggenheim, the object was a given. The addition, a thick limestone wall, recasts Wright's original composition. The new frame is vertical, rectilinear and gravitational, in counterpoint to the cantilevered bipartite composition of the original poured–concrete building.

The addition engages and integrates the large and small rotundas through a sequence of double- and single-height galleries, significantly altering the perception of the large rotunda. Instead of being the central and singular event, the rotunda is transformed into a cloister that one can enter and leave. Each ramp cycle engages the new building, providing alternative circulation options and creating an enriched perceptual engagement of the museum.

At the top of the ramp, which had previously been a dead end, the circulation sequence continues into the last of the new double-height galleries—it is no longer necessary to retrace one's steps. From the gallery it is also possible to access the roof terrace, which engages Central Park and places the entire building in the domain of its site.

The joining of the original object and the new frame were formally resolved by a "zipper wall" of glass that reveals the Wright building from both the exterior and the interior. This strategy not only reconstitutes the east facade of the original building within the new galleries, it also reveals the section of the original structure throughout.

The Opel Residence, designed in 1985, is a sequence of objects engaged, literally and formally, by a circulation spine that is, for the first time, clearly articulated as an exterior space. Thus, the framing device has been transformed—the exterior circulation system is the primary element of the formal and spatial organization of the building.

The parti responds to the clients' programmatic requirement of accommodating all three generations of their family while maintaining privacy—thus the series of interconnected "houses." These elements are organized horizontally along the arcade and are separated by a series of courtyards. In section, the arcade is an erosion under the second level of the houses. The spatial sequence is initiated at the auto court and is terminated by the entry to the main house.

The guesthouses and the main house are articulated elements that form the object/frame composition. The parabolic curve of the standing-seam metal roof creates a referential silhouette that extends the length of the building, which is then cut, creating the sequence of separate though interconnected pavilions and courtyards.

The IBM Corporate Office Building and Distribution Center, also designed in 1985, could be viewed as an extension and inversion of the Opel House. In IBM, a contrapuntal, vertical circulation entry object modulates the horizontal concrete and glass frame. If all three phases of the project had been completed, the idea of the serial object would have been realized. Of all of our buildings, it is the most primary object/frame articulation, referring to Le Corbusier's Pavilion Suisse as the diagrammatic and formal prototype.

Where the Opel Residence occupies a flat site and had a much less complex program, the Zumikon Residence, designed in 1990, is built on a sloping site. It is a building on and in the land. Like Opel, there is a series of objects and an implied frame, but the circulation spine works vertically and horizontally through the plan. The horizontal/vertical overlay and the sectional manipulation render a more complex spatial density and site organization.

The front building engages the ground with a garage and entry. An art gallery—a linear, columned space—is integrated into the entry sequence, connecting the two-and-a-half-story front entry hall to the rear stair. The front stair connects the entry level to the main living level, one level above, and establishes the volumetric aesthetic of the house.

As the house engages the land and steps up the hill, it becomes extended as a series of pavilions that are interconnected rather than consolidated. The conscious manipulation of floor planes allows one space to overview another, part of the decompositional vocabulary that clarifies the idea of the house as a series of interconnected fragments.

The curved, segmented roof forms are an elemental description of the volumes as well as a representation of the parti. The house is not read as a single object, but as a series of fragments—layered elements forming an assemblage or collage. It is a euphemistic village that anchors and establishes a sense of place and presence on the hill.

The San Onofre Residence, designed in 1993, has a binuclear parti comprising the white stucco "canyon house," a building in the ground containing the nonpublic spaces, and a "pavilion" containing the public spaces. The pavilion, with its curved limestone wall, could be read as a found object, an architectural fragment. It is separate, unique, and contrapuntal in its organization and materiality.

In addition to these two structures, designing and creating the site the site with massive retaining walls provided a unique opportunity for site integration and building organization. The site structuring and the canyon house are both informed by the Zumikon Residence, where the two are simultaneous. Where Zumikon is read as a series of erosions that result in a coherent whole, the canyon house and the pavilion are separate and distinct elements forming a collage trilogy with the site/landscape walls.

Until San Onofre, our partis were typically composites—holistic and unified. Even when we pulled the program apart and created separate indoor and outdoor spaces, as in the Zumikon Residence (or Oceanfront), the fabric of the buildings was consistent. In San Onofre, the elements are different formally and materially, while coexisting, interacting, and enriching one another. This was a breakthrough. Designing this house clarified the idea the idea of collage, fragment, and cubist composition.

The Henry Art Gallery, also designed in 1993, is like the Guggenheim in that the object, the original 1927 building, was a given and we created a frame. The Henry is more complex since our multiple addition is a fragmented collage that is clearly site-driven. It recognizes and engages the original building as a primary object, creating a much more complex, elaborated, and enriched sense of place.

Like Zumikon, the Henry engages a sloped site and steps up the hill. Counter to precedent in institutional buildings, one enters at the top and, descends, encountering progressively larger and more naturally lit space, culminating in the tripartite, curved, segmented, skylit temporary gallery.

The main gallery space is also the form/figure and primary memory of the building, which one must actually walk over or past to enter the museum. This notion of memory and referencing the iconic interplay of form, and then experiencing the space, thus realizing the sequence, is critical to the comprehensive revelation.

As with Opel, the initial linear element has been cut and eroded, leaving a series of objects with spaces between. As fragments of the solid, the skylight lanterns on the plaza remain as memories of the frame.

The Henry becomes, in its time and place, a summary that engages and recognizes all these principles simultaneously, suggesting the complexity of cross-informing one project and one programmatic response to another. That is the nature of the presentation of this monograph. Each project presents a set of clues; each is part of a process of sequential and incidental investigation that continuously infuses the work, resulting in major revelations and extensions.

The development of ideas is cross-time and cross-typology. There is, in principle, no separation between the investigation of the house and the investigation of a museum or an office building. In our mind, it is all architecture, and it is all a process to enrich and refine and, ultimately, create an essence that resolves a particular problem in a particular place.

Our new work is a speculation of the incomplete.

Zumikon Residence

San Onofre Residence

Gwathmey Residence and Studio
AMAGANSETT, NEW YORK

Building this house for my parents clarified for me that architecture doesn't have to be big to have presence or content; that a building, as an object on the land, though small (in this case only 1,200 square feet) can occupy a site with sculptural monumentality. This house, small in plan yet vertical, functions as both a piece of sculpture and a building. How it is placed and how it establishes its form is primary to its reading.

The house is composed of primary geometric forms that appear to be carved or eroded from a solid volume rather than constructed as an additive planar assemblage. The use of cedar siding on both the interior and exterior of the building furthers this reading and establishes a primary referential object. The use of the vertical siding, as opposed to shingle or clapboard, was an invention at the time, and established a primary material palette, but it was not about the materiality. It was about abstraction and establishing the form as presence. The house is unadorned and undecorated. It relies totally on the solid-void compositional integration, rather than the traditional language of house architecture.

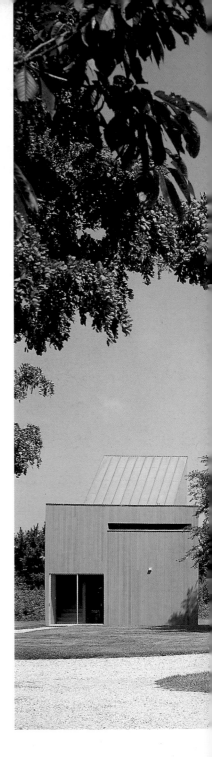

House from south over dunes | Site plan | Studio and house from south

House from northwest | North facade of house | West facade of house | South facade of house

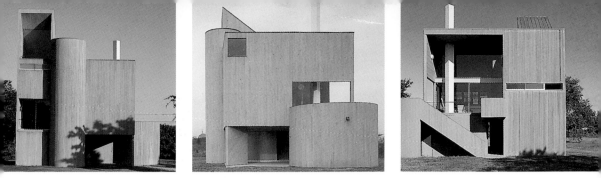

In this house, as in all our houses, it is the section rather than the plan that is the primary space definer. It is the volumetric manipulation and the vertical, rather than the horizontal, description of space that form the articulation and the definition.

The lower floor, which includes two guest rooms and a work room, is made private by the ceiling and floor above. The living level is open and the modulation occurs by the insertion of the ceiling over the dining room, above which is the studio loft. The volumetric manipulation of the space is revealed through the intersection of forms, which is further enriched by the interplay of natural light.

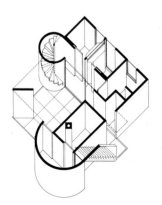

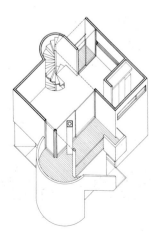

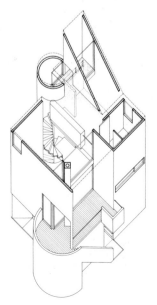

Ground-, second-, and third-level axonometrics

Raising the "public" spaces—living, dining, and kitchen—one level above grade capitalized on the views and established a relationship between the living space and the ground plane that was, at the time, unique to modern rural house architecture. By placing the continuously occupied portion of the house on a base of intermittent functions, the "parlor" floor was reinterpreted and a sense of privacy established.

Living and deck from dining | Detail at top of stair | Dining and balcony from living

Detail of south facade from balcony | House and studio from east

The addition, a year later, of a second building—a studio for my father—extended and enriched the site-object relationship. The studio's section is derived from the house, but by siting it at a 45-degree angle to the original structure a perceptual dynamic of corner versus facade was created. As you read the house frontally, you read the studio from the corner. Its objectness is immediate, three-dimensional, and contrapuntal. There is a constant interplay and dynamic relationship between the two objects. As sculptural forms, they establish a presence in the landscape, both individually and as a pair. Within the limited budget, a formal parti and vernacular were discovered that set a precedent for our later work.

Cogan Residence
EAST HAMPTON, NEW YORK

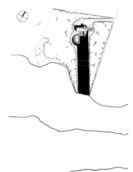

The Cogan House was our third large house. The Steel Houses, built a year earlier, had been extensions of the small-house ethic—they were primary and singular, larger versions of the carved, eroded volumetric forms of our first series of residences. We learned that expanding the vocabulary and partis of those first small houses, that making them bigger, was problematic. Extending the strategy lost the essence, the compositeness and the tension; the resulting buildings were less dynamic and less consolidated. In this house, for the first time, the "object building," with its articulated and small-scale representation, is combined with a large-scale, referential pavilion structure. The object building is locked into a frame and extended horizontally and vertically through it. The counterpoint and juxtaposition between these two elements introduced an entirely different dynamic and level of enrichment to the work.

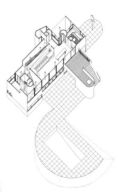

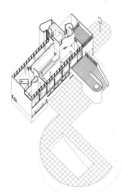

Detail of north facade | Ramp to second level | Ramp from second to third level | Ground-, second-, and third-level axonometrics

The house is sited at the top of the gently sloping site to take advantage of the panoramic views. The primary public spaces are elevated to the second level. The lower level accommodates the parking and service core (dumbwaiter and stair), the two-and-a-half story entrance porch, the foyer, the children's bedrooms, and the playroom, which was half a level below grade. The lower level constitutes the base of the "pavilion" whose "roof" becomes the new datum for the major public space above. The pavilion is supported by a columnar structure that penetrates the base building and, along with the object building, articulates the main volume.

The lower level is zoned by the entry, which separates automobile and service areas from the children's area. The entry permits direct access to the pool terrace and changing rooms and is the point of origin of the primary circulation device for the house—a ramp. The half-level landings and the linear circulation experience inherent in the ramp develop multiple and sequential spatial and view experiences.

The first leg of the ramp parallels the children's bedrooms, which, with their doors and frosted-glass interior clerestory windows, are articulated as "outdoor entries." This sense of walking past the exterior of a building is heightened by the linear skylight two and a half stories over the children's corridor and by the use of the cedar siding inside and out. The first landing arrives at the master bedroom, a modulated one- and two-story space. The second landing, above the entry and looking down through the entry portico, is the one-and-a-half-story primary living space with a large deck and outdoor stair extension. The third landing arrives at the study, a balcony over the master bedroom, with its own internal stair reconnecting it to the bedroom below.

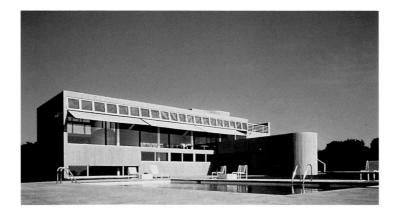

Guest bedroom and living from upper deck | South facade from pool terrace | South facade

A guest suite is reached separately, by a spiral stair from the main entry level, and has its own roof deck with views of the site, the pond, and the ocean. These multiple vertical circulation strategies contribute to the sectional complexity of the house. The half-level displacements create an overlapping section as complex and interlocked as the interaction between the pavilion frame and the object building. These sectional devices reinforce the programmatically required privacies—the master bedroom suite is separated from the children's zone and from the public spaces, while the guest suite is located at the top of the house as a roof element extending the object building vertically.

The Cogan Residence represented a major extension in complexity and compositeness that became referential for our other work. We discovered a new formal and organizational strategy for the manipulation of scale and the articulation of separate elements that are not intended to be read as singular or consolidated, but rather as "collage" and contrapuntal.

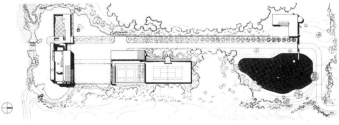

de Menil Residence

The de Menil residence involved developing seven acres on a private dune site, with access from the north, dense woods to the east and west, and a half-mile-deep dune and the ocean to the south. The arrival sequence begins with the driveway passing through the woods and a gate. Turning west, a pink stucco wall seemingly floats in a half-acre pond, a landscaped water element in counterpoint to the ocean beyond. Turning south, one passes through the stucco wall. On axis with the cobblestone drive, flanked on the west by a row of linden trees, is a long view to the ocean, a total site reference framed and abstracted by the exterior stair, brise soleil, and pool wall of the main house.

Continuing down the drive and passing the colored stucco guest house/garage, an extension of the entry-wall fragment, the full facade of the main house is finally revealed from the auto court. These three elements—the gate, the guest house, and the pool wall—constitute the series of outdoor fragments that asymmetrically establish the site architecture that frames the main house.

The house crosses the axis of the driveway and is parallel to the ocean, mediating between the land and dune sides of the site. The main facades face north, back to the property, and south, to the dunes and ocean. In plan, the house is layered north to south, in a series of four articulated and modulated zones—entry/greenhouse, circulation (the east-west organizer of the site), living, and sun-screen/brise soleil. One is constantly aware of these zones, their internal facades as well as their spatial transparency and layering. The sequential transition of spaces establishes the idea of volume as wall rather than plane as wall, a new dimension in our residential work.

Entry | Entry gallery | Living to screened porch

Accessed through a two-story entry erosion, the entry gallery is the three-story-high, skylit, cross-axial space of the circulation zone. To the right is the library, with a terrace opening to the view. Straight ahead is the kitchen/breakfast room, which is literally and programmatically the center of the house, serving the library, library terrace, screened porch, and dining room. To the left is the dining room, separated from the two-story living room by the green stucco fireplace/chimney mass, which anchors the house to the site and recalls the site walls. Both spaces are contained within and simultaneously defined and extended by the facades and volumes of the greenhouse and screened porch.

The second-floor gallery is a balcony overviewing the entry hall. To the right is the guest suite, which contains two guest rooms and decks, with views to the ocean, and a game room with its own exterior stair down to the pool terrace. To the left is the master bedroom suite including sitting, dressing, and sleeping areas as well as a master bath with a deck that is integrated into the brise soleil. Past the master bedroom, the gallery overviews the living room and expands into the study, the object in the frame of the greenhouse.

On the third level, the study loft overviews the game room, which opens to the upper level of the greenhouse. Both spaces open directly to the roof, a major outdoor space that resolves the building vertically. The chimney, skylights, and greenhouse are articulated forms that recall the spaces below, and the views of the dunes and ocean, framed by the brise soleil, recall the bridge of an ocean liner.

The brise soleil, the south facade layer, has been incorporated into the organization of the house instead of being a separate element. It is a frame that accommodates a series of objects—the screened porch, the breakfast room, the master bathroom, and a series of terraces and decks. It reads as a cornice to the site, a major scale device that establishes its presence as a piece of architecture. Like the earlier dune houses of the Hamptons, it is large enough to anchor the site and coexist with the scale of the dunes and the ocean.

Upon approach, one is aware of the volume and presence of the greenhouse, through which other interior spaces are revealed. The greenhouse is the interior garden, the extension and resolution of the landscape sequence—tennis court, garden, arbor, lawn—within the volume of the house. The three-and-a-half-story greenhouse is perceived as the major volume from the exterior and interior, a frame modulated by the intervention of the study balcony as an object. The sequence of outdoor spaces, and their extension/integration into and through the house, unifies the site and the building.

Balcony study | Balcony study from greenhouse | North facade

Opel Residence
SHELBURNE, VERMONT

The Opel residence is sited on a twelve-acre, wooded peninsula—part of the old Vanderbilt estate on Lake Champlain—with panoramic views north and west across and down the lake to the Adirondack Mountains. The clients, a retired couple who had children and grandchildren, wanted to be able to accommodate all three generations in the building. Instead of designing a single house that consolidated these different programmatic requirements, we designed a series of interconnected pavilions that allowed privacy and multiple uses.

The parti, an elaboration of the "gallery/spine" concept incubated in the Taft residence, is both program- and site-specific—it separates the guest and children's areas from the main house and affords varying lake views from all living spaces. These elements are organized along an arcade and are visually interconnected through a series of courtyard spaces. In section, the arcade is carved or eroded, rather than additive. It is cut under the second level and is terminated by the entry to the main house. It engages the different elements of the house and the exterior spaces, intensifying the overall experience of the architecture.

View from drive | Site plan | Detail of south facade from auto court

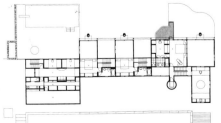
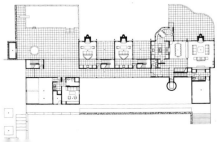

The linear circulation sequence is initiated at the auto court with the entry at the south end of a spine. To access the arcade one passes between the garage and the stair to the children's "bunk house"—a large linear, open space over the garage that the children could, over time, adjust and remake as their own environment. Walking down the arcade, one passes, sequentially, a lakeside opening that accesses the pool terrace, the caretaker's apartment, and a garden/land-side opening, with the two "guest house" entrances opposite, before arriving at the entry to the main house.

The guest houses, modeled on a European studio prototype, each contain an entry stair/hall off the arcade, a kitchen, and a two-and-a-half-story living/dining space with a vaulted roof and glazed facade that faces the lake and accommodates a fireplace/chimney object. Adjacent to each of these spaces is a private courtyard also facing the lake. The sleeping balcony overviews the living space and the lake.

The main house, on the ground level, contains a double-height entry hall, a kitchen/breakfast space, a dining area, and a two-and-a-half-story living space, similar to, though larger than, those in the guest houses. One half-level above is a studio, and on the second level is the master bedroom suite, both overviewing the living room and the lake.

Detail of studio | Living | Living | West facade (overleaf)

The section of the main house is a more complex and elaborated version of the guest houses. All read as pavilions, with the underside of the vaulted roof being the space definer. The parabolic curve of the standing-seam metal roof creates the universal silhouette of the house. This curve is extended the length of the building and then cut into segments, leaving discrete elements that are visually connected by a continuous gutter element that establishes a frame for the lakeside facade.

Simultaneously, the rhythm of the three fireplaces and chimneys acts as a vertical counterpoint to the curved roof and gutter forms. They are the stabilizing elements in the glass facades and allow the furniture to be oriented toward both the view and the fireplace. By placing the fireplaces within the glass facade, they become animated elements in a richer and larger composition that engages the landscape, lake, and mountains instead of being isolated foci and anachronistic elements in the space. From a formal and architectural point of view, their placement anchors both the space and the building.

This residence occupies a 150-foot-wide by 100-foot-deep site defined by the Pacific Coast Highway to the north and the Pacific Ocean to the south. The parti combines the row house and the courtyard house typologies, creating a hierarchy of building volumes and outdoor spaces that layer the site from north to south, resulting in a literal and psychological transformation from highway to beach.

The highway facade of the entry building is the first layer on the site. It is primarily solid, rendered as a carved, abstract horizontal wall punctured by an entry gate. It is an acoustical barrier, separating the rest of the site from the road. As a linear, horizontal figure, the facade of the entry building, with its three-dimensional modulations and articulations, suggests the presence of the different programmatic elements housed within, while simultaneously presenting a large-scale, abstract "road graphic." It is specific without being revealing; it is designed as a response to both the highway and to itself.

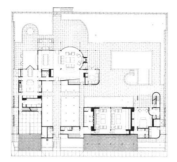 

One passes through the entry building to a courtyard conceived as a vestibule to the main house. The courtyard is planted with three rows of five pear trees that flank the path from the gate to the front door of the main house. From the entry courtyard one experiences the entry to the main house, as well as the pool terrace under the bridge, establishing a diagonal sequence of exterior spaces that are separate but interconnected.

The main house contains the living room, dining room, library, and porch on the ground level. On the second level a master bedroom, study, and decks face the ocean and overview the cylindrical double-height living—the primary interior volume and referential space of the composition. It engages all of the outdoor spaces as well as the ocean, establishing the cross-axis of the site, and becomes the mediator between the private domain and the public domains of the site.

A pool terrace extends the open space of the pear tree courtyard under a bridge that connects the main house and the entry building, where an ocean terrace links it to the beach below. Passing through this series of sequential indoor/outdoor spaces, the facades on the ocean side open up to the view and become more transparent, as opposed to solid. There is a transformation of facades—the north/road facade is closed and articulated as solid, the south/ocean facade is open and articulated as void. The idea was to establish separate elements that are programmatically articulate and engage the entire site. The site plan and the building plan are simultaneous and result in a composition that is composite, where the inside and outside spaces are integrated and form the total site composition.

This was the first house we had designed with an art collection as an integral part of the program and is, to date, our only house in Europe. The clients were incredibly acute and regarded modernism as a critical period in the history of architecture. They did not want a "house"; they wanted a work of architecture that would accommodate their family and their art. There was no hesitation, no insecurity or compromise. A reductive essentialism was a mutual mandate.

The clients collect modern sculpture, particularly the work of Richard Long. As part of their initial requirements they wanted not only to display Long's groundwork circular forms in a dedicated gallery space, but to integrate a fresco hand-painting into a major wall of the house as well. Though this latter condition did not drive the section of the living space, the idea of "wall" did become a conscious and integrated part of the design. The solid-void articulation concentrated on accommodating the art program and on creating privacy on the east and west sides of the house and transparency on the north and south.

The scheme incorporated the clients' programmatic requirements and aspirations. It also addressed the constraints posed by the stringent local planning and zoning regulations.

The first constraint, one we had never encountered with any house we had designed before, was the necessity of maintaining the existing site topography. This automatically mandated that the scheme be integrated into the sloping hillside, obviously affecting the section and, when the program was overlaid, the vertical organization of the building.

The second constraint was that the roof eave line could not measure more than 4.5 meters above the corresponding point in the land. This reinforced the relationship between the section and the topography and had a huge impact on the overall disposition of the building.

The third constraint was that the square footage of the house was determined by a proportional relationship to the area of the site. Underground space, however, was not considered part of the livable or measured space of the building.

Detail of southeast facade from service court │ Southeast facade │ Detail of southeast facade from service court

The front building engages the ground with a garage and entry. The second level, accessed by an outdoor stair from the entry court as well as by a service drive and court from the side street, contains the breakfast room and kitchen, which overview Lake Zurich and the town of Zumikon.

This building is connected to the main house by a horizontal pavilion. On the ground floor (below grade), the art gallery is integrated into the entry sequence of the house, making it experiential and obligatory in the most positive sense. It is impossible to enter or leave the house without encountering the art.

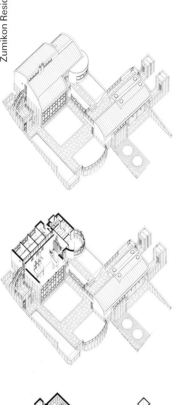

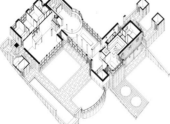

Entering the house, one understands the gallery as a linear, columned space that connects the two-and-a-half-story front entry hall to the rear stair. The front stair connects the lower entry level to the main living level, one story above. The entry space establishes, under a curved, segmented roof form, the volumetric aesthetic of the house.

The entry space engages one vertically and horizontally—vertically in section, with the entry stair balcony and upper roof, and horizontally through the gallery to the back stair—revealing the diagram of the house.

As the house engages the land and steps up the hill, horizontal spaces are created and the house becomes extended as a series of pavilions that are interconnected rather than consolidated. The conscious manipulation of floor planes allows one space to overview another. These subtle vertical shifts are part of the decompositional vocabulary that clarifies the idea of the house as a series of interconnected fragments.

On the second floor, the dining room serves as a transparent mediating space between the natural topography of the fields to the east and the man-made courtyard/roof terrace to the west. The glass-block floor, which brings natural light into the art gallery below, and the concrete columns articulate the circulation zone.

A three-story cylindrical form, which is sliced and eroded, marks the intersection of the horizontal pavilion and the main house. The cylinder contains the terminal space of the gallery on the ground floor, the music room/library (overlooking the dining room) on the second floor, and the master bedroom on the third floor

Rotated from the music room/library, the double-height living space meets the intersection of the rear stair and horizontal gallery, and opens toward the main terrace and the view of Lake Zurich and the Alps beyond. The interior space is in scale with both the terrace and the view. Its back wall, which accommodates the fireplace—a sculptural anchor to the space, both wall-engaged and floating, an alternative focus to the view across the terrace—is also the front wall to the children's house.

The clients' children had all expressed a desire to have their own domain—their own public as well as private spaces. The resolution was to create their house as a distinct element, integrated into the composition, but accessed as a separate vertical building. This was accomplished by using the rear stair, which connects all levels but engages the children's house at the half landings, physically and psychologically separating them from the main public and adult levels.

Off the master bedroom, the roof of the dining room becomes a garden terrace, planted with annual flowers. It reestablishes, in the modernist tradition, the connection between occupied land and the building. This area is part of an integrated circulation system of terraces and outdoor spaces that bring one from the lower street-level entry court up through the three levels of the house.

The curved, segmented roofs are an elemental description of the volumes as well as a representation of the parti. The house is not read as a single object, but as a series of layered elements stepping down the hill, its fragments forming an assemblage or collage. It is a euphemistic village that anchors and establishes itself on the hill.

The opportunity to build this house of reinforced concrete, given the level of craft that exists in Switzerland, was compelling and influenced the form. This is literally a building of the ground, with a density and sense of permanence that is entirely different from that of our wood-frame houses.

The materials used in this house—stucco on terra cotta for walls; lead-coated stainless steel for roofs; wood for windows and cabinetry; and limestone, sandstone, and wood for floors—produced a selective aesthetic so precise and hierarchical that it establishes the primary reading of the building and creates spaces that are inherently self-decorative.

Pool from upper terrace | Pool terrace from west

San Onofre Residence

PACIFIC PALISADES, CALIFORNIA

South facade from lawn terrace

This private residence is located on one and a half acres in a quiet residential neighborhood at the end of Malibu Canyon. A bilateral parti derived from the site's unique profile: the majesty, the quiet, the calm, the stillness, the shadows, and the density of Malibu Canyon—in contrast with the sparkling, sun-drenched horizon of daytime and the equally bright city lights at night—afforded an opportunity to design two distinctly different ideals and combine them into an architectural collage.

A three-story curved limestone pavilion housing the main living spaces is poised on a promontory looking south and east toward Santa Monica, the Pacific Ocean, and the sky-line of downtown Los Angeles. A three-story cube containing support space is embedded in the slope behind, overlooking the canyon to the west.

In addition to the two house structures, there is a third element—the site-building. Creating the site—extending the two horizontal planes at different levels—involved constructing massive retaining walls (with caissons extending 65 feet to bedrock) and provided a unique opportunity for site integration and building organization. If one removed the house from the land, the retaining walls would be a formally resolved composition, as well as a transformed ruin.

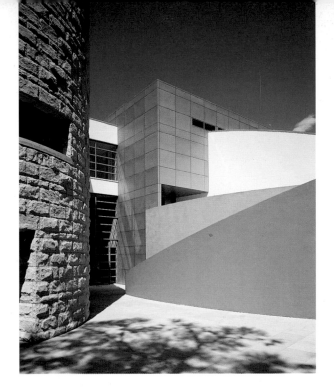

The "canyon house" was designed as a building *in* the ground, anchoring and stabilizing the pavilion, an object *on* the ground. Separate, unique, and contrapuntal in its organization and its materiality, the pavilion, with its curved limestone wall, could be read as a found object, an archeological fragment, transforming the experience of the landscape as one moves through it from the ordered programmatic distribution of the canyon house.

The canyon house is embedded in the ground and is organized vertically and bilaterally. Contained in the light-filled perimeter that overviews the canyon are the exercise room on the ground level, the children's bedrooms on the entry level, and an office/conference suite on the upper level. In the core, a screening room and a library occupy the ground level; storage and service areas are behind the garage on the entry level; and, on the upper level, the master dressing room and bath, opposite the offices, are on axis with the bridge that connects to the pavilion and the master bedroom.

Detail of the south facade from lawn terrace | Ground-level entry terrace | Exterior stair connecting entry terraces

The sequential unfolding of the site begins upon entering the house through a link element. Whether one enters on the main level or on the lower ground level, views of the canyon through the stair, and of the ocean through the pavilion, are immediately revealed. At that moment, the integration of the site is revealed, and the intersection of the stair and the bridge reconciles the vertical and horizontal connection of the two elements. The link is the volumetric lock.

Living | Dining | Detail of upper-level bridge and skylight | Upper-level bridge from dining | Master bedroom from dining

The core of the pavilion, housing the master bedroom on the upper level and the kitchen on the entry level, floats within the limestone perimeter wall. It is an object in a frame, a fragment of the canyon building that has been pulled through, forming the complex volumetric element that separates the double-height living and dining spaces. The breakfast room penetrates the screen of the brise soleil on the south glazed facade and creates an outdoor terrace extension off the master bedroom above.

At ground level, the entertainment room—the base of the core element— mediates the stone wall as an object in the frame, which, in turn, defines a covered terrace that opens to the southern lawn and accesses the swimming pool and spa facing the canyon.

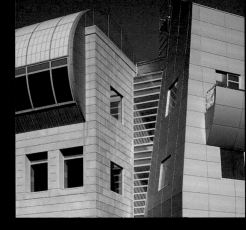

IBM Corporate Office Building and Distribution Center

Morgan Stanley Dean Witter & Co. World Headquarters

Walt Disney World Contemporary Resort Convention Center

Stadtportalhäuser

EuroDisney Convention Center and Hotel

The David Geffen Company Building

Located adjacent to a main Greensboro highway, this 145,000-square-foot office building and distribution center is the first phase of a proposed three-phase, 450,000-square-foot project.

To provide maximum flexibility in the floor plates, the elevator and stair cores are located in the entrance tower on the south facade. The structure is reinforced concrete, cantilevered from interior columns to the perimeter. On the south facade, the concrete floor planes extend to act as integrated sunscreens, adding depth to the recessed glass curtain wall. On the north facade, the glass is set flush with the concrete floor edge, inviting a contrapuntal reading. Three different types of glass express floor, sill, and suspended-ceiling elements.

Detail of brise soleil | Entry plaza and lobby | Model of proposed three phases

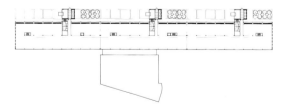

Entry plaza, south facade, and lobby | Ground- and typical-floor plans | South facade and elevator core | Porthole view from elevator stops

In contrast to the exposed concrete frame, the entrance tower is clad in white tile, glass block, white metal panels, and glass. The five-story, balconied tower reads as an object against a frame, defining the entry plaza and the landscape between the building and parking area. On the tower's solid face, square punched windows at each floor level align with the circular windows of the elevator cars, recalling the circulation sequence.

Aside from the distribution center, this was a generic loft office building with the mandate that the tenant floor be as flexible as possible. By pulling the elevator core/lobby element outside the facade, an image for the building is rendered that is in counterpoint to the south-facing sunscreen, and each floor is relieved of the primary circulation mass, allowing one to enter each floor at a single referential point. Leaving the floors, visitors get views of the city and once again find themselves in a volumetric space, in contrast to the rest of the building. Treating the lobby in this manner takes the notion of vertical circulation out of the plan, making it, at once, an object and a volume that is site- and building-referential.

Morgan Stanley Dean Witter & Co. World Headquarters

NEW YORK, NEW YORK

The design of this fifty two-story office building, located on the west block-front of Broadway between 47th and 48th Streets, reflects the aspirations of a traditional skyscraper to present an appropriately scaled public building at the pedestrian base and a strong silhouette on the skyline. The exterior forms respond to both the diagonal of Broadway and the orthogonal Manhattan street grid. The base responds to the diagonal, and the segmented curve of the double-height mechanical floor creates the transition from the rotated base to the orthogonal tower. The changing quality of natural light on the building produces images of both opacity and reflectivity, of fluidity and permanence.

West facade from the Hudson River | Broadway signage | Detail of facade

The grand lobby that runs from 47th to 48th Street is a sweeping expanse broken only by two huge, round columns. The walls are finished with gray granite accented by stripes of dark green polished marble. Other materials include white, black, and dark green marble in a geometric pattern on the floor, and a coffered ceiling of wood.

The interior design extends to executive offices, dining and meeting spaces, and boardrooms on the 40th and 41st floors, to the main lobby at street level, and to a cafeteria on the lower level.

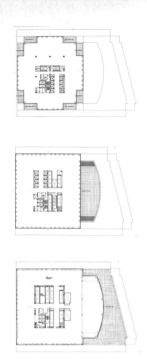

A large opening in the lobby floor accommodates escalators, stairs, and an access "bridge" that visually engages both the cafeteria and the lobby through a new curved glass wall. The horizontal and vertical spatial layering adds a new dimension and volumetric interplay that transforms the basement, a space with negative perception, into an environmentally dynamic, complex space.

This former storage area is transformed into a dining environment that can accommodate five hundred people. Once the circulation sequence of lobby, bridge, escalator, and cafeteria is experienced, the memory of the basement is eclipsed. The sequence is reinforced by both the extended materiality of the lobby and the meticulous attention to detail, lighting, and circulation clarity.

Walt Disney World Contemporary Resort Convention Center

LAKE BUENA VISTA, FLORIDA

The Contemporary Resort Convention Center is an addition to Walt Disney's visionary Contemporary Hotel, completed in 1971. A new two-and-a-half-acre entry plaza links the two buildings and leads to a new porte-cochere entry for the hotel.

Four major forms create a collage-assemblage: the curved, striped primary volume of the main ballroom and prefunction gallery; the entry canopy; a skylighted outdoor porte-cochere for cars and buses; and the two rotundas. The Convention Center's horizontal silhouette, reinforced by a strong color palette, contrasts with the vertical, gridded facade of the hotel.

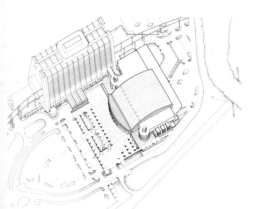

The opportunity with relation to the existing hotel was that the connection into the south rotunda—across a glass-block bridge to a balcony overlooking the major prefunction space, and down an escalator and stair to the main level—animated the rotunda with a circulation intervention and inherently made it specific to both its relationship to the meeting room and also to the existing hotel.

The main prefunction space acts as a second lobby to the auto drop-off and becomes the representative space of the form of the building—with the circular skylights, which one remembers from the roofscape and the section of the room, it becomes a major volume that accesses not only the main ballroom but also the other perpendicular prefunction spaces. It is intentionally animated in terms of its form, its color, and its full architectural articulation. The color and the graphic of the building comes through this space, rendering the space an interior/exterior extension.

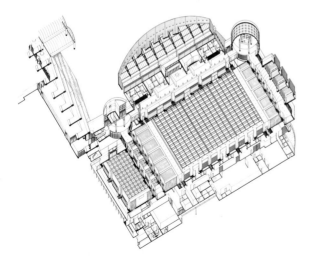

Interior axonometric viewed from below | Detail of north facade | Main ballroom

The Convention Center has an overall clarity that reflects a simple parti. Located at the center, the 45,000-square-foot main ballroom, capable of accommodating 3,300 people and of being divided into three multipurpose spaces, is flanked by meeting rooms at either end. The main entry and prefunction spaces are layered across the front of the building, and the kitchen and support areas are at the rear. Natural light, color, and texture mark primary and secondary circulation systems and articulate major program elements.

The north rotunda, accented by square punched windows, is an iconic form on the more visible west corner and provides an initial take on the entire addition. The punched windows, which at night have a very graphic reading, are transformed on the inside because they become the lighting for the space. There is no question that one sees this form when passing by or arriving at the exterior. Then, when one comes to it as part of the circulation sequence, it becomes the memory anchor of where one is on the site and an orientation reference to the entire complex.

This gateway project is located at the intersection of a major boulevard into the city of Frankfurt and the edge of a large international exposition center. The design produced a compelling plan graphic and massing collage of varying scales and multiple images.

The complexity and volumetric configurations were specific responses to the site and program, which includes a museum and office building for the Bosch Corporation, two speculative office buildings, and a hotel. The design resolution was influenced both by the importance of maintaining the site trees and an open park space and by the presence of the existing railroad bridge, road system, and exposition structures.

The silhouettes viewed from a distance and the memories elicited by the architecture as a whole are reinforced by the more immediate experiences at grade and the complexities of land and building intersections. Essential to the project's composition and image are the two similar wedge-shaped office buildings whose facades define the gate, and the dissimilar masses that extend from these facades to either side of the boulevard.

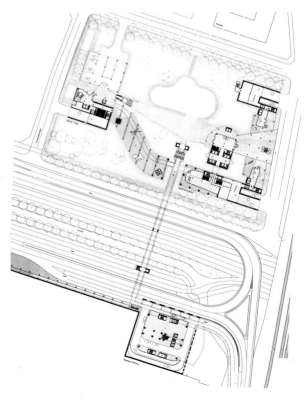

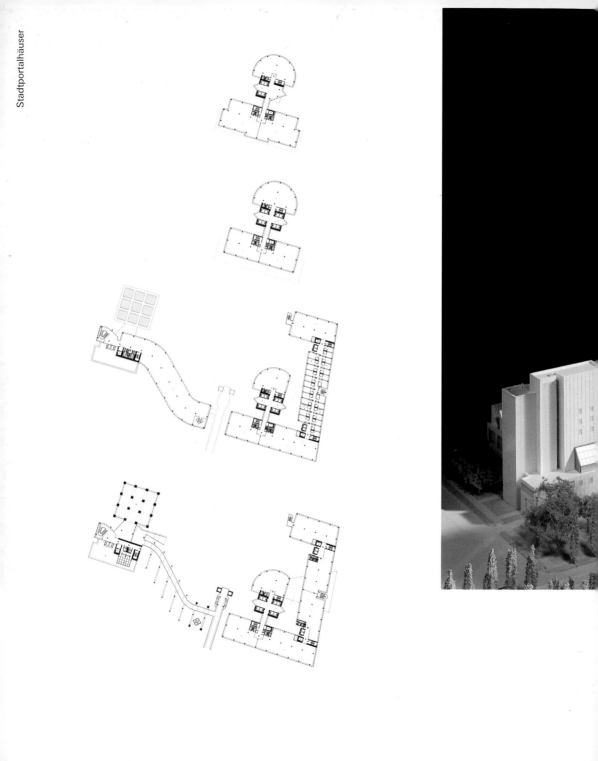

Second- and fourth-level plans of north-site office building, museum, and hotel; typical upper-level plans of north-site office building

Aerial view of model from south | Plans of south speculative office building

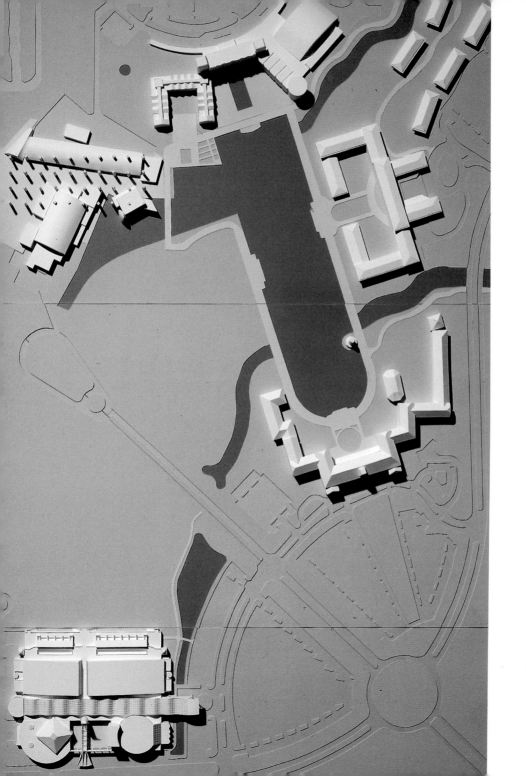

EuroDisney Convention Center and Hotel

MARNE-LA-VALLÉE, FRANCE

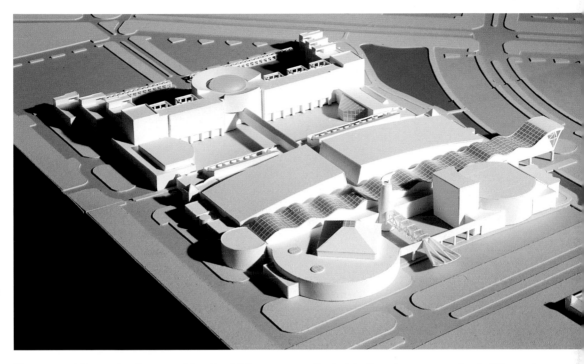

The proposed Convention Center and Hotel is a 750-room convention hotel with restaurants, meeting facilities, and a health spa, all with direct access to a 300,000-square-foot, multidimensional convention center that contains a 2,000-seat industrial theater, exhibition pavilion, ballrooms, lecture theater, meeting rooms, and full food-service facilities. It is the largest single building project at EuroDisney to date.

Located at the entrance to the EuroDisney complex, the new building departs from the decorated-box theme of surrounding hotels and presents itself as a collection of silhouettes and facades that explore the relationship between exterior form and interior volume. The sequential ordering and integration of exterior spaces, transitions, and circulation organizes the interior and articulates a constantly varying silhouette and massing, resulting in a mutable assemblage of forms whose dynamism is reinforced by the addition of color coding.

Site model | Aerial view of model from entry road | Elevation

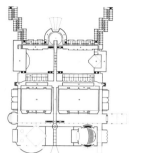
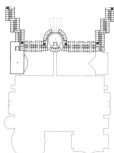
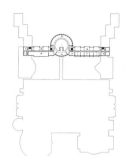

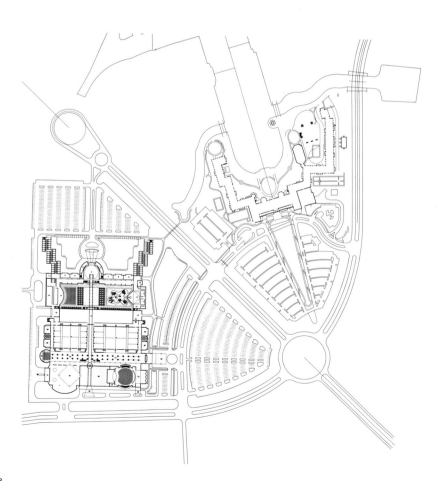

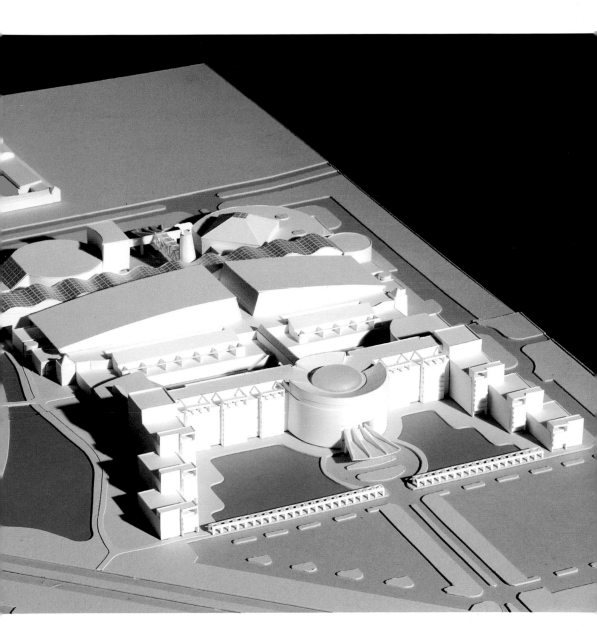

The David Geffen Company Building

BEVERLY HILLS, CALIFORNIA

This 90,000 square-foot corporate headquarters is located in the Beverly Hills Industrial District, where the zoning restrictions limit the height of buildings to three stories. The typical cornice line along the street is reinterpreted by a cylindrical translucent skylight running the length of the building and incorporating the third-floor executive offices.

Site and program variants are exploited to create a complex, hierarchically asymmetrical building. The screening room marks the garage entry and ramp; conference rooms occupy a tower at the corner, adjoining a plaza and a fountain. The main entrance space counterpoints the long facade as a concave gallery rotunda. The three-story conical shaped atrium is the central volume in the composition.

Screening room and corner entrance from southwest | Corner plaza from southeast

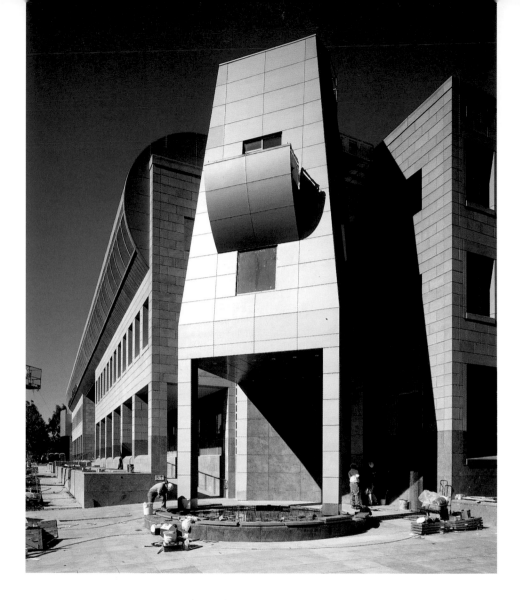

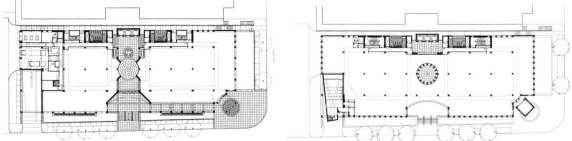

Corner tower and fountain from southeast | Ground-, second- and third-level plans

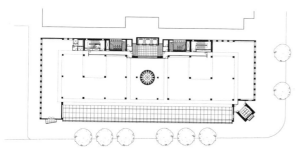

Main entrance from southwest | Detail of corner tower skylight | Arcaded ramp from the east

The primary volume is clad with a combination of textured gray limestone and green granite in contrast to the zinc metal panels of the screening room, conference tower and elevator core. The industrial steel window system has a powder coated finish and is glazed with blue/green tinted and translucent glass. The railings, exterior trim and concierge desk are stainless steel.

Detail of cylindrical Kalwall skylight at third-level office space | Longitudinal section through atrium

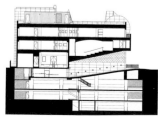

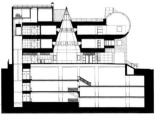

Detail of atrium | Transverse sections through screening room, west tenant, and atrium

Theory Center at the College of Engineering, Cornell University

Social Sciences Building and Computer Center, UCSD

The Science, Industry and Business Library

Nanyang Polytechnic

James S. McDonnell Hall, Princeton University

Levitt Center for University Advancement, University of Iowa

View of south facade from campus | Original east facade

In 1970, the wood interior of Whig Hall was gutted by fire, leaving only the exterior walls. The architects' response to the multiple challenges posed by the building's reconstruction was surprising and radical for its time.

Whig and its identical twin, Clio Hall, were originally built to house the university's eponymous debating societies. With Nassau Hall, an eighteenth-century administration building, the two temples form an axial composition framing Cannon Green, in the heart of the campus. As the university has grown, much of its building and student life has been concentrated to the south. By mid-century, Cannon Green had come to serve primarily as part of a system of shortcuts linked to the major route of cross-campus travel by an informal diagonal path to the east of Whig.

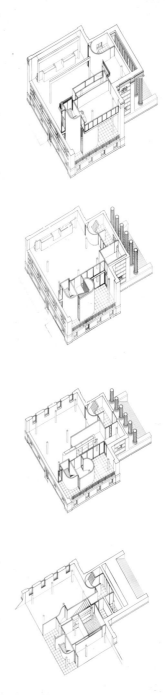

Princeton saw the restoration as an opportunity to strengthen ties of its formal center to current student use. The design solution was the creation of a new facility that is structurally and aesthetically independent from the shell of the original building, within which it sits. To avoid overburdening old walls and foundations, new full-height columns were threaded through the existing structure onto newly created foundations within the old building's perimeter. A new roof system featured a concrete tension ring to brace the entire shell at its cornice and a pre-tension break at the east. By removing the east wall, the new structure and the activity within is visible to students walking along the busy cross-campus path to the east.

Detail of south facade | Detail of stair | Ground-, first-, second-, and third-level axonometrics

Flexible meeting room from mezzanine | Flexible meeting room | Detail of stair | Detail of stair | James Madison room on top floor

The program called for 10,000 square feet of space where there had been 7,000. It required facilities not only for the debating society but also for activities relevant to a broader spectrum of students—most importantly, the office of the student president and a large meeting room to be used for lectures, movie screenings, dinners, receptions, and debates. Also to be included were an information center, a lounge, and conference, seminar, and work rooms. The offices of Whig and its private lounge, the James Madison Room, were to be rebuilt and integrated into the new building in a way that would allow them a degree of independence from the other activities being brought into the structure. Furthermore, new construction had to conform to current building codes and be fitted with a modern air-conditioning system.

Twenty-five years after designing the renovation to Whig Hall, we were asked to make the building handicapped-accessible. The addition of the circular elevator tower is consistent with and confirms the original intervention. Like the stair penetrating the roof in the original, the new tower extends through the wall. The original frame is engaged vertically and horizontally.

A round elevator cab is enclosed within a vertically cantilevered cylinder that is intersected by the glass-walled rectangular extrusions of the the floor slabs. The bridge allows the original marble wall to be read as a continuous element and provides striking views of the building's exterior and the campus.

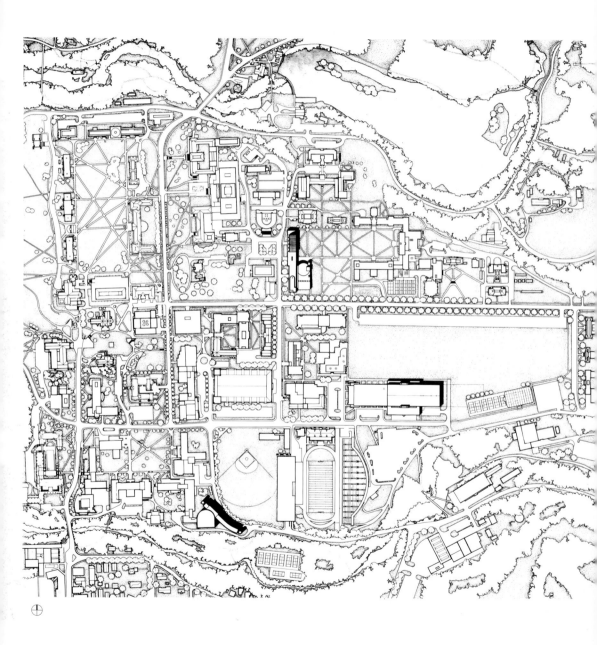

North campus site plan | School of Agriculture from quadrangle | Fieldhouse and Basketball Arena from Schoellkopf Field | Theory Center from Campus Road

At the time we began these three projects, the president of Cornell University, Frank Rhodes, was critical of many recent buildings on campus and had become the leading advocate for a new architectural sensibility and awareness. At our recommendation, the dean and a faculty member from the School of Architecture were appointed for the first time to the Cornell Architectural Review Committee.

All three buildings on the north campus—the School of Agriculture, the Fieldhouse and Basketball Arena, and the Theory Center at the College of Engineering—share common elements. They are larger than adjacent buildings, they address the issue of edge and define major outdoor spaces, and they establish precedents for a master plan that supports the urban constraints and constructs of each site.

The School of Agriculture building closes the quadrangle at the end of its west axis and forms a gateway from the south campus to Bailey Plaza, which has been redefined as an outdoor pedestrian court that anchors the main campus auditorium and adjacent structures. The Fieldhouse and Basketball Arena is an addition to the hockey rink that redefines the edge of the practice fields at the center of the north campus. The Theory Center is contextually more complex than the other two buildings, as it borders a gorge that posed significant ecological constraints. It is located on the curve of Campus Road, facing the baseball field, and is diagonally opposite the football stadium and the existing field-house, the two largest structures on campus.

With the completion of the three buildings, a precedent for Cornell University architecture was realized: site-responsive, programmatically flexible, materially dense, and scale-sensitive buildings. In their formal articulation, contextual interaction, and use of collage, these new structures are intended to read simultaneously as extensions and transformations.

School of Agriculture
CORNELL UNIVERSITY   ITHACA, NEW YORK

A user-intensive reevaluation of a previously rejected scheme for the site initiated the design process for the School of Agriculture. The rejected design, basically a mid-rise office building, was insensitive to specific site and program constraints.

Open-ended on the long (west) axis facing Bailey Plaza, the Agriculture quadrangle was defined by five-story masonry buildings on three sides. The new Administrative building, fronting both Bailey Plaza and the Agriculture quad, redefines Bailey Plaza as an urban space, and the quadrangle as an enclosed outdoor room. The building houses administrative offices on the first three floors and the Landscape Architecture School on the fourth floor. Crowning the building is a barrel-vaulted studio space with double-height windows facing the quadrangle and a framed roof terrace facing Bailey Plaza. A connecting bridge provides access to the Landscape department from the Academic building and frames a three-story gate to the quadrangle that recalls similar college gates on the campus.

Entry gate from Bailey Plaza | East facade from quadrangle | Landscape Architecture studio terrace overlooking Bailey Plaza

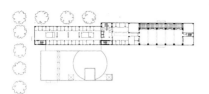

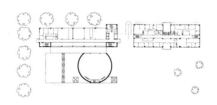

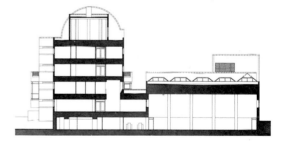

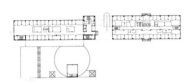

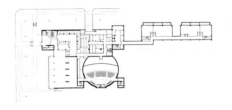

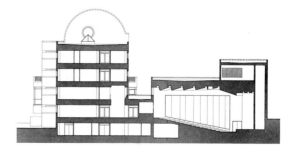

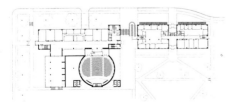

A double-height gallery with a balcony mezzanine is the primary interior circulation space. It links the two entrances and provides access to classrooms, a 600-seat lecture auditorium, and a 400-seat dining facility. The third and fourth floors contain faculty offices and teaching-support space.

On the exterior, modular brick in three shades of earth tones borrows from the texture of adjacent campus buildings. The windows are teak, with cast-stone sills and copings, and the barrel-vaulted roof is clad in standing-seam lead-coated copper.

The four-story building addresses the pertinent issues of a major campus structure—context, material, scale, and image—in a manner that supports both a new program and the traditions of the school.

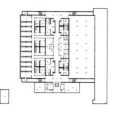
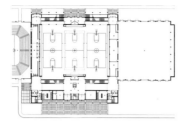
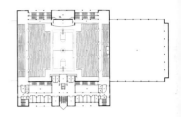

Forming the southern edge of Cornell's varsity practice fields, the Fieldhouse and Basketball Arena establishes a new image for athletic facilities on campus. Future plans include a natatorium and indoor tennis courts to the east that will complete the southern built edge, recognizing and reinforcing the quadrangle's historical role as a referential outdoor space in campus architecture.

The fixed dimensions of the basketball courts and the fieldhouse cage impose a set of given volumes arranged in the central zone of the building, aligned with the existing hockey rink. Supporting spaces are grouped symmetrically north and south of this zone, and transitional circulation spaces connect the three principal sports fields.

Whereas most of Cornell's athletic buildings are fieldstone with limestone trim, this building is constructed of ground-face concrete block, white porcelain panels, and precast concrete. The varied colors and formal articulation of the different elements form a large-scale composition that can also be read as a subtractive graphic in dialogue with the surrounding stone buildings. Unlike the traditional campus model, this architecture clearly articulates the interior volumes that define the spatial and organizational hierarchy.

Circulation spaces layer the exterior, creating recessed porches and covered entrances for pedestrians on the north and south facades. Symmetrical, monumental stairs on the north porch mirror interior stairs in the two-story skylighted lobby. The lobby, the organizational fulcrum of the building, links the office-service areas with the main athletic spaces and provides an interconnecting public entrance to the hockey rink. The central, axial stair turns on a glazed landing that projects beyond the facade, providing views and sheltering the entry below. As in our other Cornell buildings, the articulation of vertical circulation is given a logical and a strongly expressive interpretation.

The building comprises two major volumes: a basketball arena with three regulation NCAA courts and roll-out seating for 5,000 spectators, and the fieldhouse-cage. The three courts merge to form a single exhibition court when the two-tiered bleachers are extended. A continuous balcony surrounds the arena at the upper-bleacher level. At one end, an alumni lounge overlooks the court through a bay window; at the other end are coaches' offices. The balcony volumes create an object-frame notation, transforming the scale of the arena walls. The cage is a large, naturally lit multipurpose sports practice space that includes a climbing wall for teaching and training.

Fieldhouse and climbing wall | Basketball arena | Competition basketball court

Theory Center at the College of Engineering

CORNELL UNIVERSITY ITHACA, NEW YORK

The seven-story Theory Center occupies an imposing site that parallels Campus Road and borders the Cascadilla Gorge at the southeast corner of the College of Engineering. The building defines a new threshold to the campus and, though considerably larger in scale than the existing engineering facilities, establishes a new architectural image for the College of Engineering, an image previously characterized by porcelain and glass curtain walls from the fifties, without overwhelming its neighbors.

The Theory Center is composed of a linear office building and an intersecting larger cylindrical laboratory building. The laboratory building responds to the College of Engineering's long-range master plan by providing over 100,000 square feet of flexible space to systematically accommodate varying laboratory needs within the college, while entire departments are temporarily relocated for existing building renovations.

The principal entrance is located asymmetrically in the continuous facade of the office bar, at the intersection of the two primary plan forms. The facade's elevation incorporates large-scale openings, enclosed balconies, and an oculus, forming a portico and a point of reference in the outdoor movement system that organizes this edge of campus.

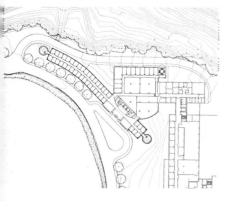

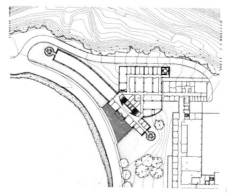

Site and typical floor plans | Aerial view from Barton Hall

Beyond it, visitors discover the volume containing the building's lobby, core, and central vertical circulation. Vertical movement is also emphasized by the egress stairs that are distinctly articulated as glazed towers at either end of the linear plan, a formal punctuation of the parti providing breathtaking views of the site topography as it drops to the lake. The towers are a rereading of an architectural tradition at Cornell, where the towers of earlier campus buildings form a pattern of symbolic punctuation unifying the campus as a whole.

The Theory Center exterior's facing materials combine alternating bands of gray brick and ribbon windows in the office bar and reddish-brown brick with punched windows in the more solid laboratory wing. This choice of materials makes connections with the larger campus setting and responds to the long views of the building from other parts of the university. It also creates an integrated palette of materials that emphasizes the volumetric interplay of the building's component parts.

Detail of stair tower, faculty office building and laboratory building | Laboratory building from service drive | Laboratory building from gorge

Social Sciences Building and Computer Center

UNIVERSITY OF CALIFORNIA SAN DIEGO LA JOLLA, CALIFORNIA

The Social Sciences Building and Computer Center was a two-phase project: first the Social Sciences Building, then a future site in the master plan for the Computer Center extension. The linear facade of the Social Sciences Building reinforces Campus Walk, the primary north-south pedestrian circulation through the campus, yet is open at the base. This provides a view through the bottom of the building down the slope and across to the mountains beyond, and engenders a sense of porosity between this major outdoor green space and Campus Walk.

The north facade of the Computer Center is specific to the faculty offices, having views of the ocean. The tilted window panels therefore render it unique to the complex as iconic and as a gateway either to or from Campus Walk.

Computer Center office addition from northwest | Computer Center office addition from west

Computer Center office addition with conference room tower from south | Detail of entrance to offices | Site/ground- and second-level plan

The black tile tower takes the black tile trim around the bay window frame articulations and uses it as a volumetric articulator. The tower contains three levels of computer training rooms, which purposely have no natural light. The tower becomes an object in the courtyard and the symbolic articulation of the building. Its roof is a terrace with ocean and mountain views.

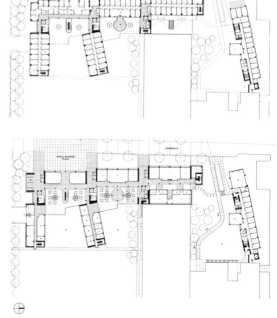

Since the building is not air-conditioned, using cross-ventilation and taking advantage of the ocean breezes was integral to its organization and design. Every office has operable windows, a fan, and transoms over the doors that can be opened. The materiality is stucco, tile, and metal used as an articulation in the fenestration system. However, the idea is to render the building as if it is carved back—the whole facade is animated as a horizontal banding and as a layering of surfaces that animate it and describe the environmental considerations.

Circulation | Corridor detail | Detail of entrance to Computer Center addition | Computer Center office and entrance

Perpendicular, and rotated off the east side of the linear building are a series of wings containing faculty and student offices, creating a series of courtyards. The existing computer building—a 1960s white stucco box—anchors this assemblage. The existing building was given a new facade and used as an exterior space-maker. It was added to and covered over on the Campus Walk side, but its existing L-shape was retained on the north side. Each courtyard is unique and creates a referential orientation toward the outdoor space between these wings, while retaining its relationship to the primary circulation spine of the entire complex.

The Science, Industry and Business Library

NEW YORK PUBLIC LIBRARY   NEW YORK, NEW YORK

Filling seven floors of the landmarked B. Altman Building in midtown Manhattan, SIBL is the New York Public Library's largest undertaking since the construction of the main building at Fifth Avenue and 42nd Street in 1911. This intervention transforms a department store designed by Trowbridge & Livingston into an interactive resource for the information age, retaining the building's classical integrity while incorporating advanced computer technologies into the infrastructure.

SIBL's window arcade invites Madison Avenue pedestrians to look into one of the few monumental public spaces in New York City with an immediate street-level impact, a two-story atrium created by removing a major portion of the existing first floor. Removing the floor creates a bridge level and transforms the typical preconception of basement, creating a new 44,000-square-foot reading space that, with the exception of the circulating library on the bridge level, consolidates all of the primary reference and staff facilities on one level. Entering from the sidewalk, one is engaged in this major volume and compelled to go down to the new ground level.

Entry from Madison Avenue | Elevator at lower level

The renovated facility reinforces SIBL's image as a "library without borders," a transparent membrane through which information and resources freely shift between the library, various business and research communities, and the public. SIBL accommodates an open-shelf reference collection, periodical shelving, catalog areas, reference specialists supported by a complete reference department, open microfilm shelving, reading areas, an electronic information center, a training center, assembly spaces, 60,000 square feet of remote storage stacks, and a full-service circulating library with storage for 1.5 million books and 50,000 square feet of administrative offices.

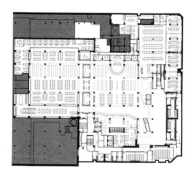

View of Healy Hall from entry bridge | Healy Hall | Entry, lower-level, and typical book stack plans

Entry hall from information desk | Typical workstation detail | Circulating library

In view of accommodating new information technologies as they emerge, flexibility and accessibility were integral to the design. One hundred computerized workstations in the Electronic Information Center provide free public access to the Internet and other electronic research tools, and five hundred stations in the Research and Circulating libraries are set up to accommodate patrons' laptop computers. The unpredictability of equipment sizes made standard library dimensions inadequate. Instead, workstations are separated by adaptable perforated dividers that offer lateral flexibility, create a definable territory, and are handicapped-accessible.

Lower-level information center | Lower-level research reading room | Research library entrance from Healy Hall

Excellent sight lines allow the entire Research Library to be supervised by five people, maximizing staffing resources. This arrangement frees the librarians from "security duty" and allows them to do specialized research or to consult with individual readers in small conference rooms. SIBL staff areas surround the stacks on the second through fourth floors, and the three uppermost levels are used for general New York Public Library administration.

A hybrid, SIBL was designed to merge the familiarity of books with the sometimes intimidating abstractions of networks and databases. The combination of traditional (stone, wood) and contemporary (stainless steel, terrazzo) materials illustrates both the humanist roots of the library-as-institution and its ability to adapt to change.

Nanyang Polytechnic

ANG MO KIO, SINGAPORE

Conceived of as a pedestrian-oriented urban village, Nanyang Polytechnic is an interactive educational community. Modeled on the University of Virginia, in the sense that there is a main iconic building, the campus extends to the north and south from the central multi-use atrium that houses common facilities.

The Administration/Student Center/Library building orients itself east and west to the major courtyards that are articulated by the lecture theater spaces in each college. Despite its size (the Administrative building alone is 500,000 square feet), the integration of courtyards and outdoor spaces, and the modulation of facades that define them, offer a variety and scale breakdown that makes the campus read more like a village than a mega-structure.

Aerial view of model from north | Aerial view of model from south | Lower-level pedestrian entry and Campus Center

Because it combines functions that are often designed as separate entities, the multi-use Campus Center/Atrium is at once economical, practical, and communal, a space that engenders dialogue between disciplines. Its complexity of program, strategic location, and spectacular presence make it an iconic destination place.

One enters on a lower level in a retail/student services/office arcade after passing a major reflecting pond on axis with the building. The scale of the entry space is monumental, establishing a critical mass and representing the importance of the institution. From this space, one can ascend escalators to pedestrian bridges, circulate through to the courtyard that accesses the student food court, or access the main theater.

A system of cloisters and covered walkways provides access to the four schools (Engineering, Health Sciences, Business Management, and Information Technology) as well as to all administrative and common-use facilities. The circulation system integrates covered outdoor terraces and is designed to form a series of landscaped outdoor spaces, gardens, and courtyards that offer a multiplicity of visual references and a sense of orientation.

The daily process of arrival, circulation, and return provides a sequence of varied visual and functional experiences. The organization of the campus integrates architecture, outdoor space, and pedestrian circulation systems in a way that is psychologically uplifting and inspirational. Circulation is conceived of as a circular loop system with no dead ends. Multiple options are available, but the primary route from the main entrance to all facilities is direct and logical.

James S. McDonnell Hall

PRINCETON UNIVERSITY PRINCETON , NEW JERSEY

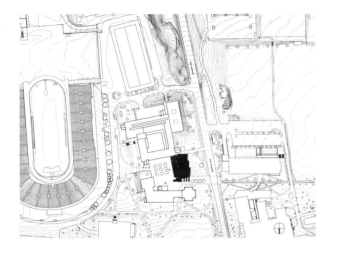

Princeton's new undergraduate physics building defines the fourth corner of the intersection of the primary automobile approach to campus and a major cross-campus pedestrian axis. It also forms a visual and physical link between the existing Jadwin and Fine Halls, which had previously been separated by an under-used plaza that put an abrupt, arbitrary end to College Walk. By joining the two buildings and enclosing the plaza, which will eventually be relandscaped, a math and physics cluster is formed, resolving incompatible building scales and site complexities.

Three major programmatic divisions—lecture halls, class-rooms, and labs—are articulated as discrete elements in their massing and materiality. Compressed partially below grade, two teaching theaters form a brick "base" for two building "objects." A cast-stone volume, housing classrooms and service areas, trans-forms the existing plaza into a more defined courtyard. A zinc-clad element housing labs and flexible teaching spaces is rotated to resolve the different geometries of the two adjacent buildings and to provide a frontal orientation to College Walk. The barrel-vaulted roof over the labs, visible from the taller adjacent build-ings, is treated as a fifth facade.

Ground-and basement-level plans | Lecture theater stairs from College Walk | Stair from landing | Stair from entry

From College Walk, a double-height canopy marks the two main entrances. This canopy and the other public circulation elements weave through the building, connecting the various programmatic elements to each other, and with Fine and Jadwin Halls, the Plaza, and College Walk. The entrance at grade serves the labs and classrooms on levels one and two. The rotation of the labs creates a series of wider corridor areas for displays, chalkboards, and waiting students.

An exterior stair leads down to a second entrance that allows public access to the lecture halls and library after hours, and lets hundreds of students going to lectures bypass the quiet classroom areas. This entrance accesses a 6,000-square-foot gallery below the plaza that is both a connection between the existing buildings and a lobby area for the two new lecture halls, and is capable of accommodating up to 1,000 students during class changeovers.

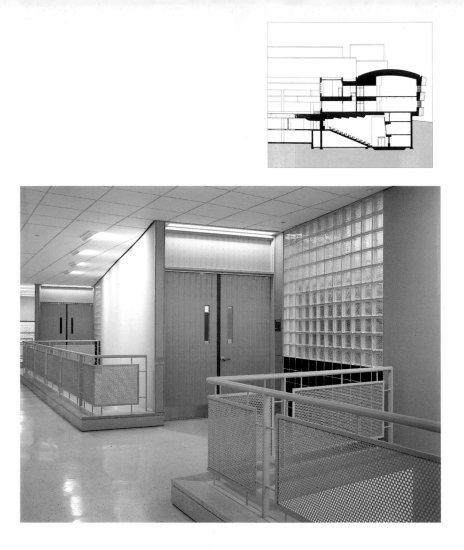

One of the most challenging aspects of the project was the design of the new lecture halls, which had to accommodate unique features for teaching undergraduate physics and be flexible enough to be used for other university functions. Twenty-four-foot-diameter turntables were installed at each stage, allowing experiments, some of which take several days to set up, to be rotated back-of-the-house while other presentations are being made. Rear projection screens permit higher audience light levels, allowing students to simultaneously observe experiments and audiovisual programs. Concealed catwalks thirty feet above the stage are used to launch, drop, and swing objects to demonstrate natural phenomena, one of the hallmarks of Princeton's teaching method.

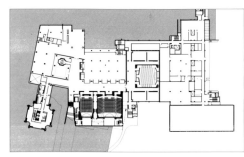

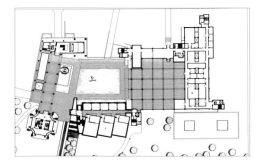

The building's exterior palette was chosen to engage the Jadwin/Fine complex and the two Venturi buildings across Washington Road in a dialogue. The exterior base is clad in alternating bands of black manganese iron-spot brick and gray wire-cut brick, recalling the black accent brick and taupe stucco used in Lewis Thomas Hall, as well as the granite used in Fine Hall. The striped pattern continues the bold graphics of the Venturi buildings while picking up the scale and texture of Jadwin's brick. The taupe cast-stone of the classroom "block" reinforces the color and texture of Fine Tower. The most visible part of the building is sheathed in standing-seam zinc panels and zinc shingles, or scales. The zinc used on the exterior walls is carried up onto the standing-seam roof, further articulating the lab element as an "object."

Levitt Center for University Advancement

UNIVERSITY OF IOWA   IOWA CITY, IOWA

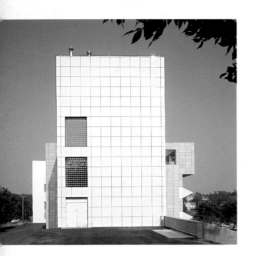

Visible from many parts of the city—particularly at night—the Levitt Center, clad in white metal panels, glass block, and Indiana limestone, is an asymmetrical assemblage of geometric forms that articulate a hierarchical sequence of public gathering spaces and private work areas.

The building is an inversion of the typical configuration of public spaces on the ground level with offices above; here office floors act as a pedestal for major public spaces that overview the campus, river, and park. The five-story rotunda, the exterior of which marks a visual and literal edge to the university's Performing Arts Campus, anchors the complex and acts as its main public meeting and circulation space.

West facade | Southeast across Iowa River | Rotunda

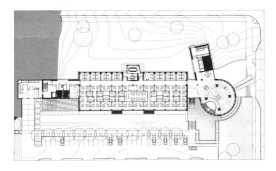

Rotunda and circulation core from northeast | Typical and fourth-level plans | Main entrance | Atrium at main entrance

The three-story interior of the rotunda is a "vertical lobby" encircled by a ceremonial stair and cantilevered bridges that create a promenade, leading visitors to the assembly spaces at the top of the building. This atrium space integrates numerous works of art by faculty, students, and local artists.

    South facade | Section | Meeting rooms | Detail of south facade

The top floor of the building's bar element contains three "peaks"—double-height assembly halls that are rotated to provide views of the river. The rotation creates a series of connected but distinct solids, and a series of discrete areas on the roof terrace. The three rooms can be combined into one, seating approximately 1,000, or can be divided and used simultaneously for different functions such as receptions, lectures, or dinners. The sculptural forms of these rooms distinguish their public functions from the three floors of administrative offices below and define a "cornice" to the arts campus.

A double-height, circular boardroom "caps" the rotunda. This flexible space, with an inverted dome ceiling, features sophisticated audio/video equipment and concentric, cherry and stone conference tables. A portion of the rotunda is carved to create a private covered terrace with views of the river and theater.

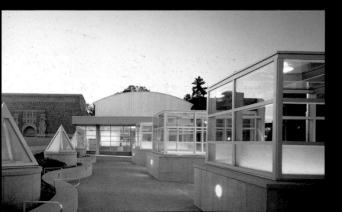

Guggenheim Museum Renovation and Addition

NEW YORK, NEW YORK

The renovation of and addition to the Solomon R. Guggenheim Museum comprises 51,000 square feet of new and renovated gallery space, 15,000 square feet of new office space, a restored theater, a new restaurant, and retrofitted support and storage areas. The original structure—through the fourth floor of the small rotunda, the existing annex, and the fifth and seventh floor double-height galleries—is now entirely devoted to new exhibition space.

The addition refers directly both to Frank Lloyd Wright's proposed annex of 1949–52 and to the former William Wesley Peters annex, initially designed as a ten-story building. Existing annex columns on the fifth floor were extended vertically to accommodate the addition. At the triangular stair, the new volume provides balcony views and access to the rotunda from three new double-height galleries and one single-story gallery. The transparent glass wall between the monitor building and the addition reveals the original facades from both the outside in and the inside out.

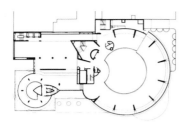

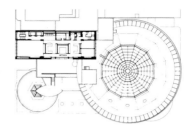

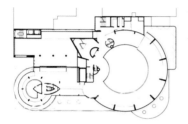

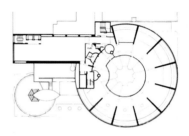

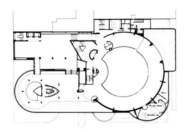

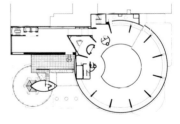

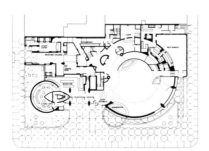

Detail of north facade | Ground- through fifth-, seventh-, and eighth-level plans | Section through addition and monitor building

Frank Lloyd Wright originally intended the large rotunda and adjacent two-story gallery to be the only exhibition spaces. The monitor building was to accommodate administrative, library, and other related functions. The two opposing spatial organizations—the ascending spiral ramp and domed skylight of the rotunda, and the horizontally stacked "prairie house" pavilions of the monitor building—were internally separated. However, when the Thannhauser Collection was donated in 1954, the second floor of the monitor building was renovated as permanent gallery space, which established the precedent for spatial interconnection between the monitor building and the large rotunda. We extended this precedent by converting each floor of the monitor building into exhibition gallery space and by integrating the pavilions, functionally and spatially, with the large rotunda.

Now integrated both functionally and spatially with the large rotunda and the new addition, the interconnected pavilions offer views to Central Park and to the skylighted small rotunda. Outside, the new fifth-floor roof sculpture terrace, the large rotunda roof terrace, and the renovated public ramp reveal the original building in a new extended and comprehensive perspective.

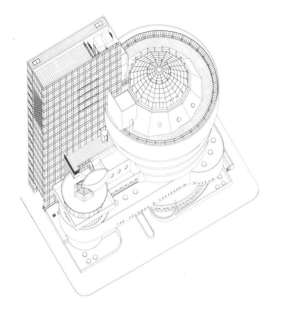

Axonometric | New fifth- and sixth-level gallery with access to new roof terrace | New roof terrace showing intersection of large rotunda and addition

Within the rotunda, numerous technical refinements have corrected omissions in the original construction and brought the building up to current museum standards. The reglazing of the central lantern, the re-opening of the clerestories running between the turns of the spiral wall, and the restoration of the scalloped flat clerestory at the perimeter of the ground-floor exhibition space have recaptured the quality of light evident in Wright's original design. The high gallery set the original precedent for leaving and reentering the ramp/rotunda. Each ramp cycle now affords the option of entry or views to new galleries. Most significantly, the extension of the uppermost ramp of the rotunda, which had been closed to the public since it was built, creates alternative circulation back to the ground floor and provides a culmination for this major public space for the first time.

The major exterior material is limestone, chosen for its immediate contextual references both to Fifth Avenue and adjacent neighborhood buildings and for its complementary relationship to the original structure.

Designing a new addition to the 1927 Fogg Museum on the eastern edge of the Harvard campus presented both structural and contextual challenges. The program required new permanent exhibition galleries, a changing exhibition gallery, study archives, administrative offices, and a fine arts library. The addition had to negotiate between the neo-Georgian Fogg (whose style prevails on the Harvard campus) and its canonical modern neighbor to the southwest, the Carpenter Center for the Visual Arts—Le Corbusier's only North American work.

Rather than competing with Le Corbusier, the solution refers first and foremost to the Fogg's formal organization. One side of the peripheral circulation of the existing museum's courtyard now extends into the new building, connecting the two major massing elements of the design.

South louvered window from gallery | East entry facade from Prescott Street

Werner Otto Hall, Busch-Reisinger Museum/
Fine Arts Library Addition to the Fogg Museum

HARVARD UNIVERSITY   CAMBRIDGE, MASSACHUSETTS

1988 | 1991

Fogg Museum and south facade of addition from Carpenter Center ramp │ South facade from Carpenter Center

To the north are the primary spaces: the library reading room on the ground floor and the permanent collection galleries on the second floor. The two-story volume extends the central axis of the Fogg to Prescott Street, where the new building presents its primary facade. To the south are support and smaller-scale spaces: the library staff offices, the temporary exhibition gallery, and the study archives. These spaces are organized in a three-story element, set back from the street and rotated to address Carpenter Center.

Ramp and entry plaza from Prescott Street

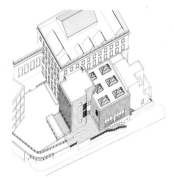

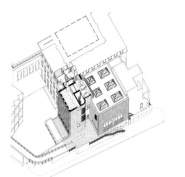

Entry/introduction gallery to Busch-Reisinger Museum | Ground- through roof-level axonometrics | Fine Arts library reading room | Permanent collection galleries

The new design also resolves Le Corbusier's compelling site circulation idea. The Carpenter Center ramp, originally intended to provide a public walkway through the building from Quincy Street to Prescott Street, ended abruptly in the Fogg's rear yard. Now the path of the ramp extends onto a new plaza, from which the public can choose to enter the library or descend a new exterior stair to the street.

Limestone, porcelain metal panels, and green granite make up the exterior, offsetting both the monolithic concrete of Carpenter Center and the brick and limestone of the Fogg.

Study room in archives | Pyramidal skylights on gallery roof | East facade from corner of Prescott Street and Broadway

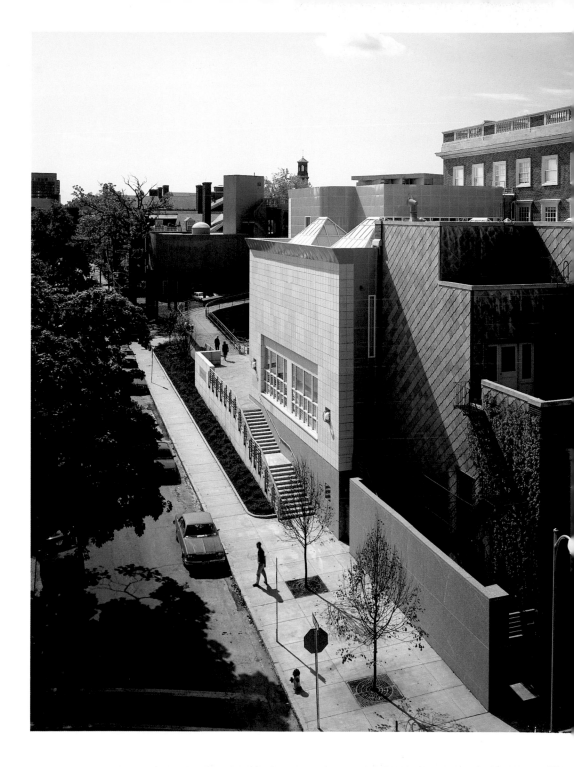

Museum of Contemporary Art
NORTH MIAMI, FLORIDA

The creation of a contemporary art museum in a mixed commercial and residential pocket of North Miami transfigured a parking lot into an animated destination point and redefined the downtown area as a cultural center.

Part of an urban revitalization project, the publicly funded museum mediates between City Hall and Police Headquarters, providing pedestrian circulation to every part of the trio of civic buildings. MOCA appears at the back of a wide public plaza, prefaced by a grid of palms, a large reflecting pool, and a versatile pavilion used for concerts and other performances, films, installations, and art education programs.

Entry from public plaza | Site plan

Four articulated and interconnected "objects," rendered in earth-hued stucco, concrete and glass block, galvanized corrugated-metal panels, and steel, combine to form an intense visual collage that invites visitors to engage with art and architecture. The emphasis on community interaction evinced by the generous public space leading up to the museum continues within. The use of simple, everyday materials such as concrete and corrugated metal imparts an accessibility, suggesting that art is meant to be experienced, used, incorporated into one's life—rather than mutely and passively observed.

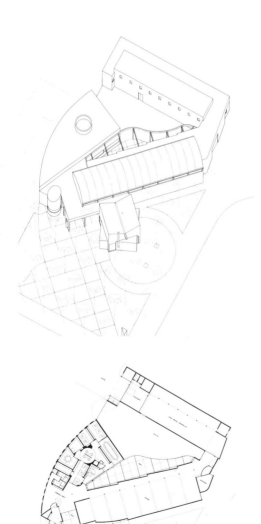

Axonometric and floor plan | Detail of west facade | East facade with museum store and entry arcade

Such approachability voices an implicit institutional critique, and is crucial for a museum determined to fuse community outreach and recognition of regional artists with international art on the cutting edge. MOCA's permanent collection encompasses works by such established artists as Dan Flavin and Louise Nevelson, local figures like Teresita Fernandez and Jose Bedia, and younger, emerging artists such as Dana Hoey and Anna Gaskell. Special exhibitions have put pressure on questions of canon formation and consensus making.

In counterpoint to the original Henry Art Gallery, the new main gallery constitutes a memorable form to be re-experienced from within. The addition acts as a carving away of a solid, revealing fragments that interact with the existing 1927 Carl F. Gould building to resite it as the asymmetrical, though primary, object in a new contextual frame—a reinterpretation of the never-completed beaux-arts museum complex.

The intervention is an architectural collage that unifies disparate elements in both contrapuntal and asymmetrical variations. The variations reestablish the primary site axis, reconcile the vertical transition from the street to the plaza level, and integrate the original Henry facade with the new sculpture court and gallery entry and as well as the campus entry.

The new three-story addition offsets the original structure with textured stainless steel, cast-in-place concrete, and cast stone. It houses versatile top-lighted galleries, administrative offices, and loading, storage, and conservation spaces, as well as a new lobby, museum store, and lecture theater. Perhaps most important, the intervention visually separates the museum and addition from adjacent structures, affording a legitimate transition, a new sense of place, a suggestive and enriched entry sequence, and an integration of site, circulation, and context.

Aerial view from 15th Street ⏐ View of original building and addition from 15th Street

Site plan and section | Sculpture court | New sculpture terrace | View east from pedestrian bridge (overleaf)

A 10,000-square-foot, two-story masonry structure, the original Henry was overwhelmed by large neighboring buildings and compromised by an existing pedestrian bridge. The pedestrian bridge was reoriented to align with Suzzalo Library at the heart of the campus, and the site lowered at the existing entry to create a sunken sculpture court. The excavation of the sculpture court allowed the original first floor to function as a piano nobile and the lower level to be perceived as being at grade rather than as a basement.

The solution begins with a linear volume behind and parallel to the original building, situated between it and an existing underground parking garage. To ease pedestrian site penetration, and to preserve axial views from Campus Parkway to Suzzalo Library and the statue of George Washington, a portion of the linear structure is "compressed" below grade. This compression leaves fragments or traces in the form of three skylights, which articulate the gatelike porosity of the site and bring natural light to the administrative offices below. The remainder of the building pushes forward to the street under a curved, skylighted roof, like a "foothill" to the campus.

Plaza, looking north toward new entry | East facade from campus | New entry from George Washington Lane

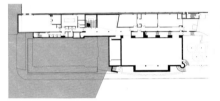

Double-height East gallery with Richard Long mural | Middle-level circulation area overlooking East gallery | Looking northeast

Depending on the circulation route taken through the museum and curatorial usage of the various gallery spaces, the East Gallery can function independently, housing a separate small show, or as either an introduction to or summary of the exhibit in the Main Gallery.

Middle-level circulation area overlooking East gallery | Looking south

Main gallery stair from lower-level | Main gallery stair from middle-level | Sections | Main gallery at stair

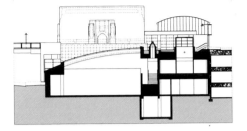

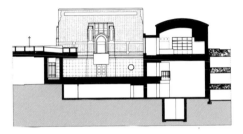

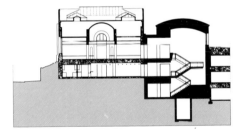

As one descends the cascading main gallery stair and emerges into the gallery—a space that has been previewed from the topmost landing of the stair—there is an inversion of expectation: rather than becoming smaller and darker, the building becomes more spacious and light-filled.

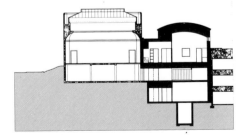

The luminous cylindrical shaft at the core of the exterior spiral stair anchors the southwest corner of the main gallery and the site. As fragments, the exterior forms of the building imply but do not directly reveal their spaces; anticipation, sequential revelation, and memory are as crucial to the experience of the complex as the physical manifestation.

Photography Credits

Peter Aaron/Esto
Morgan Stanley Dean Witter & Co. World Headquarters
Photographs on pp. 99 (top), 100 (top), 101 (top), 101-102
The Science, Industry and Business Library
All photographs

Assassi Productions
Henry Art Gallery, University of Washington
Photographs on pp. 222-223, 226-237
Oceanfront Residence
All photographs
San Onofre Residence
All photographs except pp. 81 (top), 82
Social Sciences Building and Computer Center, UCSD
Photographs on pp. 154-156, 158 (top)
Levitt Center for University Advancement, University of Iowa
Photographs on pp. 184 (bottom), 185, 188 (top), 189-190, 191 (bottom), 192

Steven Brooke Studios
Museum of Contemporary Art, North Miami
All photographs

Richard Bryant/Arcaid
IBM Corporate Office Building and Distribution Center
All photographs
Opel Residence
All photographs
Zumikon Residence
All photographs except pp. 74 (bottom), 74-75

Anita Calero
San Onofre Residence
Photograph on pp. 81 (top), 82

Jeff Goldberg/Esto
Fieldhouse and Basketball Arena, Cornell University
Photographs on pp. 147 (bottom), 148-149
Morgan Stanley Dean Witter & Co. World Headquarters
Photographs on pp. 98, 99 (bottom), 100 (bottom), 101 (bottom)
School of Agriculture, Cornell University
Photographs on pp. 138, 140, 142-143
Guggenheim Museum Renovation and Addition
All photographs
Walt Disney World Contemporary Resort Convention Center
All photographs

David Hirsch
Gwathmey Residence
Photographs on pp. 16, 19 (center), 20-21, 22
Whig Hall, Princeton University
Photograph on page 129

Hewitt/Garrison
Social Sciences Building and Computer Center, UCSD
Photographs on pp. 157, 158 (left and right), 159-161

James F. Housel
Henry Art Gallery, University of Washington
Photographs on pp. 224-225, 238-239

Tim Hursley
School of Agriculture, Cornell University
Photographs on pp. 137, 139, 141
Fieldhouse and Basketball Arena, Cornell University
Photographs on pp. 137, 144-145, 146, 147 (top)
Theory Center at the College of Engineering, Cornell University
All photographs

Albert Lim
Nanyang Polytechnic
All photographs

Mancia/Bodmer
Zumikon Residence
Photographs on pp. 74 (bottom), 74-75

Norman McGrath
de Menil Residence
All photographs except pp. 219, 223 (top), 227 (bottom)
Gwathmey Residence and Studio
Photographs on pp. 16-17, 18, 22-23
James S. McDonnell Hall, Princeton University
All photographs
Whig Hall, Princeton University
Photographs on pp. 128-129, 130-135

Richard Payne
Levitt Center for University Advancement, University of Iowa
Photographs on pp. 184 (top), 186-187, 188 (bottom), 191 (top), 193

Jock Pottle/Esto
EuroDisney Convention Center and Hotel
All photographs
Stadtportalhäuser
All photographs

Roberto Schezen
Gwathmey Residence and Studio
Photograph on page 17 (left and right)
de Menil Residence
Photograph on page 39 (top)

Ezra Stoller/Esto
Cogan Residence
All photographs

Paul Warchol
Werner Otto Hall, Busch-Reisinger Museum Fine Arts Library Addition to the Fogg Museum
All photographs